Anne's glory box

Gloria McKinnon

Distributed By
Quilters' Resource Inc.
Chicago, IL 60614
1-312 278-5695

Happy Stitching Wendy
Gloria McKinnon

Contents

The Story of Anne's Glory Box

Over the last eighteen years, Anne's Glory Box has evolved from its simple beginnings in the industrial city of Newcastle into a craft phenomenon, known around the world.

Anne's Glory Box was opened in 1976 by Anne O'Brien and I (hence the name). Originally, the shop stocked quality lingerie, gifts and linens for the glory box or hope chest.

After some years, Anne retired. The original philosophy of 'giving people what they want' was married with a new philosophy – 'make it yourself and make it better'. Soon a classroom was added to the shop and I began to teach classes.

I had been embroidering since the age of eight. As children, we were not allowed to say we were bored as long as there was gardening to be done. Instead, I asked my mother and my aunt to teach me embroidery. I've always loved flowers, but they were always too slow to come up and flower for my liking. For impatient people like me, a friendly local florist is a necessity.

I had already been teaching classes in the use of cosmetics so I thought teaching needlework and crafts shouldn't be too difficult. Little did I think that it would lead to a career which included teaching in Australia and three or four times a year in the United States as well!

It was a group of my friends, meeting each week to make Christmas ornaments and decorations, who gave me the confidence to add that classroom. Soon, I was invited to demonstrate a Christmas ornament on television and now I have a regular segment every two weeks.

Anne's Glory Box has also built a close relationship with many international teachers of needlework and crafts. This resulted largely from one of life's happy accidents. In 1988, I learned that Pat Kyser, a well-known teacher of patchwork, was coming from the United States to teach in Australia and that the class had to be cancelled due to a lack of venue. With only three days to go, I offered my classroom and these special classes began. As Pat tells it, 'the ball was dropped and Gloria picked it up!'.

Anne's Glory Box is a showcase for fine needlework and craft skills.

Through Pat, I was introduced to Martha Pullen, a relationship that has blossomed on both sides. Anne's Glory Box now brings the Martha Pullen School to Australia and I teach twice a year at her school in Alabama.

These days, the classes are thriving and have produced many wonderfully talented graduates. In planning the contents of this book, I was keen to showcase some of those people and their skills.

Gloria

Silk Ribbon Embroidery

Irises
Make these using 7 mm/ ⁵⁄₁₆ in silk ribbon.

Stitch the leaves and stems in straight stitches. Work an open fly stitch, then work a straight stitch through the securing loop at the bottom, allowing it to curve gently.

Wound Rose
Make these using 7 mm/ ⁵⁄₁₆ in silk ribbon and matching thread.

Wind the ribbon loosely around a pin until you achieve the required size. Usually, three or four rounds will do.

With the matching thread make tiny stitches at intervals through the ribbon, allowing it to fall and fold gently. Make sure each loop is caught in the stitching. Remove the pin and secure the centre.

Back Stitch Rose
Working outwards from the centre, back stitch clockwise in a spiral, beginning with a stitch length of approximately 5 mm/ ¼ in for the first two rounds and lengthening to 1 cm/ ½ in for the next two rounds.

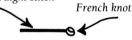

Straight stitch   *French knot*

Work the centre of the rose in pistol stitch. Bring the ribbon through to the right side at the centre of the rose, then anchor a straight stitch at the required length with a French knot. You can vary the length of the centres.

Couched Rose
This rose is also worked in a spiral from the centre with the ribbon being couched at intervals with matching 4 mm/ ³⁄₁₆ in silk ribbon. Continue making the spiral until you are pleased with the size and shape of your rose.

Violets
Work the violet petals in straight stitches using 4 mm/ ³⁄₁₆ in violet silk ribbon. Work a French knot in the centre using a gold thread.

Violet leaves are worked in blanket stitch, using 4 mm/ ³⁄₁₆ in rich green silk ribbon.

Wheat
Using 4 mm/ ³⁄₁₆ in yellow silk ribbon and beginning with a single straight stitch, continue working 'upwards' with open fly stitches.

Leaves
Groups of leaves are worked in the same way as the wheat, using 4 mm/ ³⁄₁₆ in green ribbon. Small leaves are worked with straight stitches, using 4 mm/ ³⁄₁₆ in silk ribbon.

Marigolds or Gerberas
Stitch a ring of straight stitches in a matching colour wool. Stitch over this ring with straight stitches in silk ribbon.

Work two rounds of looped ribbon stitch around the padded ring. Work French knots in the centre.

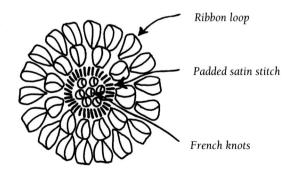

Ribbon loop

Padded satin stitch

French knots

Fuschias

Fuschias are made in 7 mm/⁵⁄₁₆ in silk ribbon in two shades of pink.

For the base, using the paler pink and beginning with the bottom layer, work two straight stitches side by side with a third straight stitch worked loosely across the bottom of the first two.

Work a floppy open fly stitch at the top in the darker pink.

Form the stamens in pistol stitch (a straight stitch anchored at one end with a French knot) in the darker pink.

Fantasy Flowers

The large blue flowers in the picture on page 29 are worked in large lazy daisy stitches with accents in straight stitches in a contrasting 7 mm/⁵⁄₁₆ in silk ribbon. Work a French knot in the centre.

The large pink flowers are worked in 7 mm/⁵⁄₁₆ in ribbon stitch, left quite loose. The centre is a wool-padded ring with French knots inside.

Primroses

Work a ring of blanket stitch in 4 mm/³⁄₁₆ in ribbon, leaving a centre of reasonable size. In the centre, work ribbon loops, anchored with French knots.

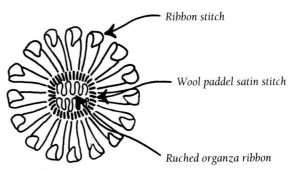

Ribbon stitch

Wool paddel satin stitch

Ruched organza ribbon

Beige Flowers

Work a ring of ribbon stitch in 7 mm/⁵⁄₁₆ in wide ribbon, having the roll on the outer edge. The centre is a wool-padded ring with ruffled 7 mm/⁵⁄₁₆ in organza ribbon.

Feather Flowers

Work loops of 2 mm/¹⁄₁₆ in silk ribbon in two rows with French knots in the centre of the rows.

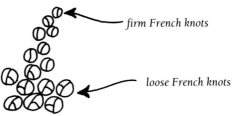

firm French knots

loose French knots

Grape Hyacinths

Using 2 mm/¹⁄₁₆ in silk ribbon, work graded French knots from loose at the bottom to very tight at the top.

Gloria's tips
for Successful Silk Ribbon Embroidery

I was first introduced to silk ribbon embroidery by Melva McCameron, an Australian living in the United States. It only took one day and I was hooked!

It is a very forgiving and rewarding form of embroidery. Forgiving because nature rarely forms a perfect flower so you don't need to either. If you make a flower you are not entirely happy with, just keep working until the picture is complete and then judge if you need to redo the flower. Most times, you will find you don't. It is rewarding because it covers so quickly that you will see results immediately.

Ribbons
As a general rule, I use Kanagawa silk ribbons in widths from 2 mm to 7 mm/ $^1/_{16}$ in to $^5/_{16}$ in. Occasionally, I use a piece of rayon ribbon that has been overdyed.

I use a knot to begin, others don't; there are no right or wrong ways to do things – just different ways.

Work with short lengths of ribbon. This page is a good length to use. When you begin, thread the ribbon through the needle, then take the point of the needle back through the ribbon approximately 6 mm/$^1/_4$ in from the end. This will allow you to use more of the ribbon (less waste) and save you searching around on the floor if the needle should fall.

Fabric
You can do silk ribbon embroidery on just about any fabric you can put a needle through. However, buy the best fabric you can afford. It takes just as long to embroider a cheap fabric as a good one but the results are very different.

If you are working on something that will need to be washed, take that into account when you are choosing your fabric.

Needles
I like to use Piecemaker tapestry needles in sizes from 20 to 26 (the higher the number, the smaller the needle).

Hoops
I always use a small hoop because I find it comfortable to do so and the work is even. Other people do lovely work without a hoop, so it is a matter of personal choice.

Wool Embroidered Flowers

Wool Rose

Use two shades of pink, one light and one dark. With the darker pink, work four straight stitches beside one another. Still using the darker pink, work another four straight stitches over the top of the previous ones.

Using the lighter shade of pink and beginning three-quarters of the way along the side, work four straight stitches diagonally across one corner of the square. The fourth stitch is very small and is almost under the third one.

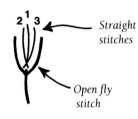

Continue in this manner, stitching over each corner of the square.

If the rose needs to be rounded out a little, moving clockwise, work small stem stitches around the outside.

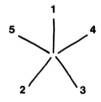

Rose Buds

Using a darker pink, work three straight stitches, with the outer two crossing over slightly at the base. Work an open fly stitch in green around the outside of the bud.

Straight stitches

Open fly stitch

Daisies

Daisy petals should always be worked from the centre outwards, following the order indicated.

Stitch each petal, using lazy daisy stitch. When the petals are complete, work a French knot in the centre.

Rose Leaves

Begin with a straight stitch and then work as many open fly stitches as you need to give a nice leaf shape.

Lavender

Baste in a curved line as a guide. Using fine wool, work five straight stitches together, then four straight stitches, then three, then two, then one.

Forget-me-not

Use these small flowers as fillers. Make each petal as small as possible.

Using two strands of blue wool and following the steps for a five petal flower, work a tiny flower with straight stitches. Work three or four stitches into the same two holes for each petal. Work a French knot in the centre.

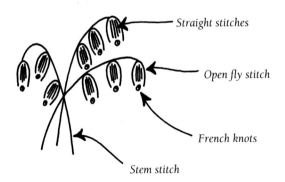

Straight stitches

Open fly stitch

French knots

Stem stitch

Lily of the Valley

Using two strands of fine white thread, work four straight stitches on top of one another. Work an open fly stitch in white so that the 'arms' extend beyond the centre stitches. Work a pale green French knot at the end of the centre stitches. Work the stems in stem stitch in pale green.

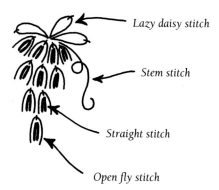

- Lazy daisy stitch
- Stem stitch
- Straight stitch
- Open fly stitch

Wisteria

Using a mushroom-coloured thick wool, work two stitches one on top of the other. Work open fly stitches around the flower centre in fine mauve wool.

Work large open leaves in green lazy daisy stitch and tendrils in green stem stitch.

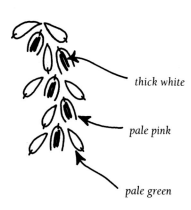

thick white

pale pink

pale green

Wisteria Blossoms

Using exactly the same stitches as for the wisteria, work the centres in thick white wool, the fly stitch in fine pale pink wool and the leaves and stems in pale green.

Iris

Work a lazy daisy stitch for the top of the flower, using two strands of fine wool. The outward leaning petals of the iris are indicated with a looped stitch through the back of the lazy daisy stitch. The loop can be worked in the same colour or in a mix of two different colours.

Work the stem with a single straight stitch in green and the leaves with long loose lazy daisy stitches.

Violets

Stitch the flower using a single purple thread. Make two large lazy daisy stitches at the top and three small ones at the bottom. Make a gold French knot in the centre.

For the bud, work a very small lazy daisy stitch in purple with a green open fly stitch around it. The stem is a long straight stitch. Work the leaves in green buttonhole stitch.

Filler Flower

This is a tiny flower that can be used as a filler, either in trails or bunches. Work two straight stitches on four sides of a small square with a French knot in the centre.

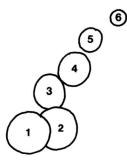

Hollyhocks

The flowers are made up of wheels of buttonhole stitch, beginning with the largest one at the bottom and adding smaller ones up to the bud at the top. Make them curve slightly.

The leaves are also worked in buttonhole stitch but the stitch does not go into the same hole each time. Place the leaves along the base of the largest flower.

The buds are three buttonhole stitches with an open fly stitch surround.

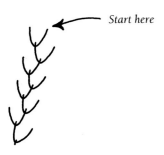

Start here

Fly Stitch Greenery

Work an interconnecting series of fly stitches, beginning at the top.

Silk Ribbon Rose

Use 4 mm/ 3/16 in wide silk ribbon in two shades of the same colour.

For the rose centres, make five French or colonial knots in the darker shade. Work two rounds of stem stitch around the centre, using the lighter shade.

For the buds, work two straight stitches, one on top of the other, then work an open fly stitch around it in green wool.

Gloria's tips
for Successful Wool Embroidery

Wool embroidery, like silk ribbon embroidery, is rewarding and forgiving. With a few tips, you can make one of the beautiful projects in this book.

Threads

Experiment with the variety of woollen threads available. In most cases, I have not specified which wool to use for a particular flower. Generally, you can choose one which suits you, the effect you wish to create, and is easily available. Some of the threads used in this book are: Appleton's Crewel Wool, Appleton's Tapestry Wool, DMC Tapestry Wool, DMC Medici Wool, Fancyworks Overdyed Wool, Royal Stitch Wool and Kacoonda Threads.

Always use a manageable length of thread. Generally, finger to elbow is the recommended length, but I have to confess, I leave it a little longer. I usually begin stitching with a knot.

Needles

You will need an assortment of needles in sizes from 18 to 24. I like to use Piecemaker tapestry needles, using the ones with larger eyes for tapestry wool and the ones with smaller eyes for crewel wool.

Fabrics

As a general rule, use the best quality fabric you can afford. The blankets in this book have been made using one hundred per cent pure Australian wool. This can be handwashed but I also wash blankets in my washing machine on a gentle cycle. Use a good quality wool wash and stay by the machine so you can stop the spin cycle before the blanket becomes felt. Spin only long enough to remove the excess water, then dry outside on the clothesline.

Transferring a Design

On the Pull Out Pattern Sheet, you will find some of the embroidery designs, given in detail. There are a number of methods for transferring an embroidery design to your fabric. Using transfer paper is probably the easiest. Simply trace the design from the pattern sheet, then transfer it using the transfer paper.

However, don't be too pedantic. This is a form of creative embroidery – so create! Use the pictures as a guide but don't worry if your flowers are in slightly different positions or are different colours. Embroider them in a way that pleases you.

Nightgown

MADE BY WENDY LEE RAGAN

This is a beautiful embroidered and lace-trimmed nightgown. It would also be the perfect gift for a mother-to-be as it has a generous front opening. As a special treat, in our next book we hope to bring you the matching peignoir to complete the set.

Materials

- ❧ 4 m/4¼ yd of white cotton lawn for the skirt
- ❧ 60 cm/⅔ yd of white Swiss batiste or cotton lawn for the yoke
- ❧ 23 cm/9 in x 45 cm/18 in of light blue Swiss batiste or cotton lawn
- ❧ 2 m/2 yd of 1 cm/ ½ in wide white edging lace
- ❧ 2 m/2 yd of 2.5 cm/1 in wide white edging lace
- ❧ 2 m/2 yd of 4 cm/1½ in wide white edging lace
- ❧ 6 m/6½ yd of 5 cm/2 in wide white edging lace
- ❧ 4 m/4 yd white entredeux
- ❧ Floche embroidery thread: F20 Light Yellow, 744 Yellow, 754 Peach, 819 Light Pink, F43 Pink, 651 Light Blue, F35 Blue, 369 Green, 415 Grey
- ❧ DMC Stranded Cotton, white, for the appliqué cord
- ❧ needles, size 7 betweens
- ❧ seven small buttons
- ❧ Madeira Tanne white cotton thread, no. 80
- ❧ white sewing thread
- ❧ universal machine-sewing needles, nos 65 and 100
- ❧ no. 2 pencil or a drafting pencil
- ❧ tracing paper
- ❧ spray starch

Method

See the Pattern, Embroidery Designs and Templates on the Pull Out Pattern Sheet.

For the yoke

1 Spray starch the white Swiss batiste or lawn fabric and press it well.

2 Trace two front yokes and two back yokes from the pattern sheet. Do not cut out these pieces but cut a rough rectangle around each shape.

3 Trace the embroidery designs from the pattern sheet and transfer the designs on to the two front yokes and one back yoke. The other back yoke piece will be the lining.

4 Embroider one left and one right front yoke, leaving the lining free. Embroider the back yoke, following the embroidery guide on the pattern sheet and the stitch guide on pages 13 and 14.

5 Wash all the yoke sections. Allow them to dry, then press well. Accurately cut out all the yoke pieces.

6 With the right sides facing, the raw edges even and using 2 cm/ ¾ in seam allowances, join the shoulder seams of the embroidered yokes. Trim the seams to 6 mm/ ¼ in and press them open. Join the shoulder seams of the front yoke linings and the back yoke lining. Trim the seams and press them open. Turn the yoke right sides out. Baste the raw neck, armhole and bottom edges together.

7 Trim the batiste from one side of the entredeux. Spray starch both the entredeux and the fabric at the bottom edge of the front and back yokes. Place the entredeux and the fabric together with right sides facing and the edge of the entredeux approximately 6 mm/ ¼ in from the fabric edge. Attach the entredeux with small zigzag stitches. Choose a stitch that places the 'zig' in the holes of the entredeux and the 'zag' in the fabric. Press the yoke and set it aside.

For the nightgown skirt

1 Cut out the following pieces:
Skirt front: 1 m/40 in x 115 cm/45 in,
Skirt back: 1 m/40 in x 115 cm/45 in, **Ruffle:** four strips 20 cm/7 in wide, cut across the full width of the fabric.

2 Trace and cut out the template for the top of the skirt pieces. Using the templates, mark the armholes for the front and back skirts. Cut out the armholes.

3 Using French seams, sew the side seams of the front and back skirts, keeping the seams 6 mm/ ¼ in or less. Press the skirt, folding the seams to the back of the garment.

4 Using a regular stitch length, sew three rows of gathering at the top of the front and back skirts. Set them aside.

5 Using tiny French seams, sew the four ruffle pieces
together to form a circle. Pintuck along the centre of the
ruffle, using a seven-groove pintucking foot. Place the tucks
in the following grouping with a space between each group:
one tuck, two tucks, three tucks, one tuck, two tucks. Press
the pintucks after each tuck.

Note: You may find it easier to stitch the pintucks if you
loosen the top tension slightly.

6 Attach the 5 cm/2 in wide lace edging by stitching in the
heading of the lace, using a small straight stitch, then
hemstitch the lace to the fabric.

Note: Use the Madeira Tanne no. 80 thread and a
no. 100 universal machine sewing needle for a prettier
hemstitch – more like handworked pinstitch.

7 Sew three rows of gathering at the top of the ruffle in the
same way as for the top of the skirt. Gather up the ruffle
to fit the bottom of the skirt, then pin and stitch the ruffle in
place. Trim the seam allowance back to 6 mm/¼ in and roll
and whip the raw edges.

For the front opening

1 Pull up the gathering on the top of the skirt to fit the
bottom edge of the yoke. Place the entredeux and the
fabric together with right sides facing, adjusting the gathering
as you go, and placing the ditch of the entredeux on, or a
little below, the last gathering line. Keep the area at the front
where the opening placket will be free of gathering. Stitch in
the ditch of the entredeux with a short straight stitch. Trim

back to 3 mm/⅛ in. Stitch with a close zigzag, stitching into
one hole of the entredeux and all the way off the fabric on the
other side. This will roll the fabric and entredeux edges right
into the entredeux.

2 Trace and cut out the pattern for the placket. Cut out the
placket from the blue Swiss batiste. Turn in and press
1 cm/½ in on the sides and bottom of the front placket,
folding in the corners diagonally. (Fig. 1)

3 Pin the right side of the long side of the placket to the
wrong side of the nightgown front. Stitch along the
stitching lines, pivoting at the small dots. (Fig. 2)

4 Cut down the placket between the lines of stitching,
clipping diagonally to the small dots. Trim the long seam
allowances and press them towards the placket. (Fig. 3)

5 Fold the placket sections along the fold line with the
right sides together. Stitch across the top edge and trim
off the excess fabric. (Fig. 4)

6 Turn the shorter side of the placket to the outside along
the fold line, placing the pressed edge over the seam.
Edgestitch close to the edge, by hand or machine, ending at
the small dot then stitch along the fold. Turn the other side of
the placket to the outside and edgestitch as before taking care
not to catch the shorter side in the seam.

7 On the outside, lap the right front band over the left
front band, matching the centres. Stitch close to the
edges below the small dots and along the stitching lines.
(Fig. 5) Pinstitch around the front bands, if you wish.

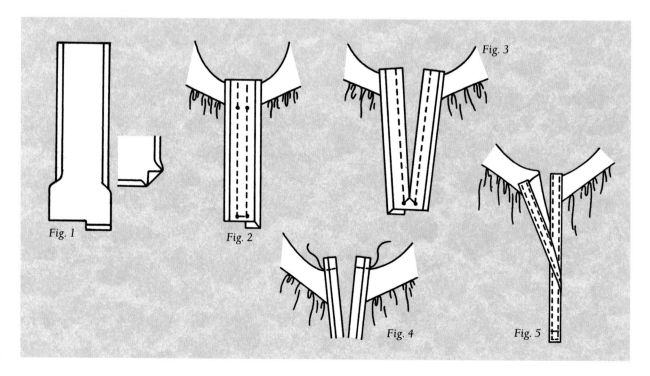

Fig. 1

Fig. 2

Fig. 3

Fig. 4

Fig. 5

8 Make seven buttonholes in the right front placket and sew on the buttons to correspond.

For the lace

1 Trim the batiste edge of the entredeux, spray starch and then sew the entredeux around the armholes as for the bottom of the yoke. Gather up the 1 cm/ $\frac{1}{2}$ in wide edging lace to fit the armholes. Sew the gathered lace to the entredeux, trim the edges and cover with a close zigzag stitch.

2 Trim and attach the entredeux and gathered lace around the neckline in the same way as for the armholes but using the 2.5 cm/1 in wide edging lace.

3 Gather the remaining 5 cm/2 in wide edging lace to fit the front yoke/skirt seam. Attach the lace by hand to the skirt edge of the entredeux with tiny stitches. Attach the lace to the back yoke in the same way, using the 4 cm/1 $\frac{1}{2}$ in wide edging lace instead.

Stitch Guide

Shadow embroidery

Use a crewel needle, size 10, and a 45 cm/18 in single strand of stranded embroidery cotton. Place the fabric in a hoop and begin with a waste knot. In shadow stitch, you form a basketweave of thread that covers the area to be filled and is surrounded by back stitches.

1 Bring the needle through at **a** and take a stitch to **b**. Bring the needle up at **c** and take a stitch to **b**. (Fig. A)

2 Bring the needle up at **d** and take a stitch to **a**. On the wrong side, carry the thread over, bringing it out at **e** and take a stitch to **c**. (Fig. B)

3 On the wrong side, carry the thread over, bringing it out at f then take a stitch back to **d**. On the wrong side, carry the thread over, bringing it out at **g** then take a stitch back to **e**. Continue in this way until the area is filled. (Fig. C)

Granitos or Rondels

These are tiny dots made by laying six or seven straight stitches over one another. They can be worked with or without a hoop.

Split Stitch

This is commonly used for padding which is covered by other stitches. It can be worked with or without a hoop. (Fig. D)

Bullion Stitches

Bullion stitches are the basis for embroidering many flowers.

1 Begin by anchoring the thread, then take a stitch from **a** to **b**, taking the needle back to **a**. Insert the needle at **b** again, just up to the eye. (Fig. E)

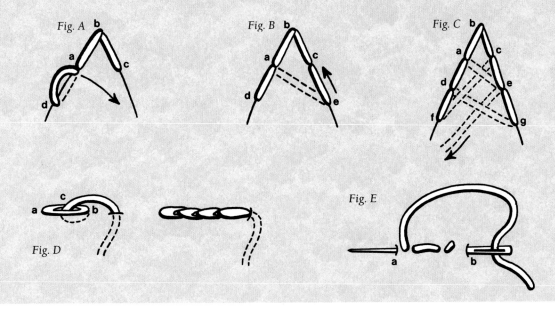

Fig. A   Fig. B   Fig. C

Fig. D   Fig. E

Stitch Guide continued …

2 Wrap the thread around the needle, keeping it close to **a**. (Fig. F). Controlling the wraps firmly with your left thumb, push the needle through and slide the wraps off the needle. Slide the wraps down the thread until they are lying on the fabric. Reinsert the needle at **b**.

Bullion rosebuds are made by laying two bullion stitches side by side. Make one of the bullions one wrap larger than the other. For a bullion rose, make three bullions side by side. The inside one is usually one or two wraps smaller than the outside ones. Here's a tip: wrap the thread around the needle until the tube is the desired length, then add one more wrap. This is to compensate for the fact that the bullion will compact when you slide it off the needle.

For bullion pinwheels, draw a circle of the desired size with a dot in the centre. Stitch around the outside with split stitches, then make bullions from the outside ring, over the split stitches, into the centre, until the circle is filled.

Shaded Eyelets

1 Draw an oval with an offset circle inside it. Outline both with split stitches. (Fig. G) With an awl, push open the threads inside the circle. Don't break the threads.

2 Inside the oval, stitch two or three layers of padding satin stitches, alternating the direction of the layers. (Fig. H)

3 When the padding is completed, satin stitch around the eyelet over the padding. These shaded eyelets can be stitched with or without a hoop. (Fig. J)

Appliqué Cord

The heart on the centre back yoke is stitched in this technique.

1 Cut a length of cord (stranded cotton) that is twice the length of the heart outline. Anchor the cord in the fabric.

2 Pinstitch over the cord until you have completed the outline of the heart. (Fig. K)

3 Bring the cord around and pinstitch over it, working back the way you came, but on the other side and using the same holes. (Fig. L)

4 To finish, overlap the cords and couch them, or bring them to the back of your work and tie them off or weave them into the stitches.

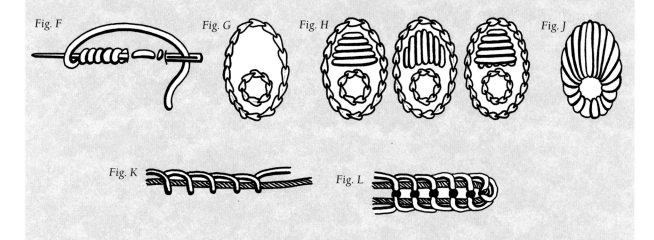

Fig. F   *Fig. G*   *Fig. H*   *Fig. J*

Fig. K   *Fig. L*

Painted Lamp

<small>PAINTED BY MEROPE MILLS</small>

This lovely folk art painted lampstand and shade will find a place in any home. Choose colours to suit your own decor or follow the colour and painting instructions given here.

Merope recommends that you buy the shade unassembled at a store which makes lampshades. Work on it flat, then when the painting is completed, return the shade to the store to be assembled.

Materials

- ♣ laminated paper lampshade
- ♣ lampstand with an electrical fitting
- ♣ graphite paper, white and blue
- ♣ stylus
- ♣ coloured chalk pencil
- ♣ tape measure
- ♣ large and small sea sponges
- ♣ flat brush, size 2.5 cm/1 in
- ♣ Raphael S8404 brush, size 2 or 3
- ♣ old plate or saucer for a palette
- ♣ Jo Sonja All-Purpose Sealer or another water-based sealer
- ♣ Jo Sonja Colors: Warm White, Teal Green, Smoked Pearl, Fawn, Burgundy, Plum Pink, Red Earth
- ♣ Matisse Professional Artists Acrylic Colour, Antique Green OR Jo Sonja Colors, Teal Green mixed with Fawn
- ♣ clear satin-proof varnish

Method

See the Painting Designs on the Pull Out Pattern Sheet.

Lampshade

Note: The right side of the shade is the shiny side.

1 Mix together Antique Green and Smoked Pearl to make a pale green. Add a little water to the mixture.

2 Wet the larger sponge and squeeze out any excess water. Dip the sponge into the paint and sponge the shade on the right side from one side to the other. Leave it to dry, then sponge the back of the shade. Leave it to dry.

3 On the right side, measure 6.5 cm/2¾ in from the bottom edge of the shade. Mark a line, using the chalk pencil, all the way around to the other end.

4 Using the 2.5 cm/1 in flat brush, paint the border in Antique Green. Leave it to dry, then apply a second, then a third coat – leaving it to dry between coats. Test the border to make sure it is opaque and not streaky by holding it in front of a switched-on light bulb. If there are any streaks, apply another coat.

5 Where the border meets the sponged part of the lampshade, paint in a scalloped border in Warm White.

For the leaves

1 Trace the leaf design from the Pattern Sheet on to the Antique Green border using the white graphite paper and a stylus. Use the coloured graphite paper for the leaves which go beyond the border into the sponged section. Repeat the design along the shade, making four clusters of leaves.

2 Using the size 2 or 3 brush, paint the leaves in a mixture of Teal Green and Antique Green, making them darker than the border. Paint them from top to bottom with smooth, regular strokes until you have covered the entire leaf. Paint the veins and detail of the leaves in Teal Green.

For the flowers

1 Trace in the large flowers in the same way as for the leaves. Do not trace in the daisies. Base coat the large flowers in Smoked Pearl, blocking out the leaves. If required, apply a second coat after the first coat is dry. Take care that the painting is smooth and has no ridges. Trace in the detail of the individual petals and centres.

2 The flowers are painted in the three following colour mixes and you can alternate the colours in each posy:
First colour: a mixture of Plum Pink and Fawn, with a touch of Warm White. The centre is Burgundy.
Second colour: a mixture of Red Earth and Fawn, with a touch of Warm White. The centre is Red Earth.
Third colour: a mixture of Smoked Pearl, with a touch of Fawn. The centre is Burgundy.

Paint the centre flower in the first posy in the first colour, paint the flowers left and right of the centre flower in the second colour, then paint the flower on the far right side in the third colour.

3 Squeeze out Warm White on to your palette. Load the size 2 or 3 brush with thick Warm White, flattening the brush in the paint. Carefully pull the paint down towards the centre of the flower, working from the outer edge of each petal. Clean your brush and gently blend in the white by smudging the paint where the two colours meet. Repeat the process for the bottom petals.

4 Paint in the appropriate colour for the centre and again blend where the two colours meet.

5 Paint in the stamens which fan out, then add little white dots at the end of each one.

For the daisies

1 Paint the daisies in a mixture of Fawn and Warm White. You can paint these freehand, referring to the design for positioning.

2 Twirl the brush into a point in the paint. Pick up a dot of paint and pull little commas straight into the centre, working in a circle to form the daisy. Add a Red Earth dot for the centre. Outline the petals in Warm White. Add trailing sprigs. Paint commas to represent buds in shades of Fawn, Red Earth and Warm White. Allow to dry thoroughly.

Finishing

Wet the small sea sponge and squeeze out all the water. Squeeze the sealer out on to a palette. Dip the sponge into the sealer and work with even movements from the top of the shade to the bottom and from one end to the other on the right side of the shade. When the sealer is dry, apply a second coat, leave it to dry, then apply a third coat. Seal the back of the shade with two coats of sealer.

Lampstand

Repeat the posy twice on the bottom of the stand and paint it in the same way as the lampshade. Varnish the stand with two coats of clear varnish.

If you would like some additional information about Merope's style of painting, the following books might be useful:

❦ *Imaginative Brushwork*, Milner Craft Series
❦ *Victorian Lace & Roses*, Heirloom Project (Elladvent Pty Limited
❦ *Hollyhock Cottage*, Heirloom Project (Elladvent Pty Limited)

Floral Garden Blanket

STITCHED BY FAY KING

This charming little blanket would be perfect for a new baby. Choose embroidery wools (DMC Tapestry Wool, Appletons Crewel Wool and overdyed wools) and silk ribbon to complement the colours in the fabric you use for the backing.

Materials

- ❧ 56 cm x 80 cm/22 in x 32 in cream blanket wool
- ❧ 1.2 m/1⅓ yd Liberty print fabric for the backing and the ruffle
- ❧ matching sewing thread
- ❧ an assortment of Piecemaker tapestry needles, sizes 18-24
- ❧ handsewing needles
- ❧ a variety of wools and silk ribbon
- ❧ 12 mm/½ in wide rayon ribbon for the bow
- ❧ tailors chalk

Method

See the Embroidery Guide and the Bow Outline on the Pull Out Pattern Sheet.

Embroidery

1 Fold the blanket wool in half widthwise and lengthwise to find the centre. Mark this point.

2 With the tailors chalk, draw an oval, 25 cm x 46 cm/ 10 in x 18 in, centred over the middle point. Baste in the outline of the oval.

3 Embroider the flowers, using a variety of wools and silk ribbon, following the embroidery guide.

4 The posts are worked in stem stitch, using a single strand of wool. The paving is worked in large open fly stitches. It looks particularly effective when it is worked in variegated wools. (Fig. 1)

5 Make the small bows with 4 mm/¼ in wide silk ribbon. Form a loop on one side and couch it in two places. (Fig. 2). Make a matching loop on the other side. Close the centre with a straight stitch. The bow tails are straight stitch with a couple of small straight stitches worked at right angles to the tails.

6 For the large bow, tie a bow using 12 mm/½ in wide rayon ribbon. Attach the bow to the blanket, using French knots. Thread the tails of the bow through the blanket and fasten them with French knots as well.

Assembling

1 Cut six 10 cm/4 in wide strips for the ruffle across the full width of the fabric. Join the strips together to form a circle. Press the ruffle strip over double with the wrong sides together.

2 Gather the ruffle with two rows of gathering. Pull up the gathering then pin the ruffle around the right side of the embroidered blanket wool with the raw edges even. Adjust the gathering to fit. Stitch the ruffle in place, 1 cm/½ in from the blanket edge.

3 Cut the backing fabric to the same size as the embroidered blanket wool. Place the backing and the embroidered piece together with right sides facing and the raw edges even with the ruffle sandwiched in between. Stitch 1 cm/½ in from the edge, leaving a 15 cm/6 in opening in one side and taking care not to catch the fullness of the ruffle in the stitching. Turn the blanket through to the right side and slipstitch the opening closed.

4 Press the blanket on the backing side over a large fluffy towel to protect the embroidery from being pressed flat.

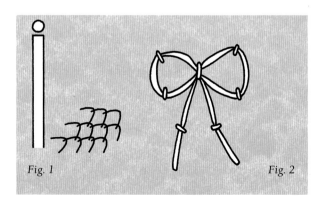

Fig. 1   *Fig. 2*

Seven Sisters Quilt

STITCHED BY FAY KING

This quilt design has been popular for more than a hundred years. Made in this way, it is not a quilt which is usually recommended for beginners as it does require a little experience to piece it accurately.

It is very important to ensure your templates are traced precisely from the ones given on the pattern sheet so that your quilt comes together well.

In our quilt, each star and border is cut from a different Liberty print fabric – a total of seventy-three different fabrics. For simplicity, it is possible to piece each hexagonal unit from the same seven fabrics and one background fabric.

This quilt has been handpieced by the English method, using cardboard throughout, and handquilted.

Finished size: 133 cm x 150 cm/52 in x 60 in

Materials

- ❧ scraps of seventy-three different fabrics
- ❧ 1.5 m/1²/₃ yd of white homespun for background
- ❧ fineline permanent marker pen
- ❧ template plastic
- ❧ scissors
- ❧ medium-weight cardboard
- ❧ sharp pencil
- ❧ transparent ruler
- ❧ masking tape
- ❧ handsewing needles
- ❧ strong matching sewing thread
- ❧ approximately 145 cm x 160 cm/58 in x 64 in of backing fabric
- ❧ approximately 138 cm x 156 cm/55 in x 62 in of wadding
- ❧ quilting thread

Method

See the Templates on the Pull Out Pattern Sheet.

Cutting

Cut out the following pieces:
For each star: six of template A in floral fabric.
For each hexagonal unit: seven stars (forty-two of template A in floral fabric, thirty of template A in the background fabric and six of template B in the background fabric, six of template C in the colour of your choice) and piece them.
For the quilt top: four each of templates D, E, F and G from the background fabric.

1 Trace template A from the pattern sheet on to the template plastic, using the marker pen. Cut out the template along the marked line.

2 Using the plastic template A and the sharp pencil, draw around the template on to the cardboard. Cut out the cardboard templates in the numbers you require.

3 Place the plastic template A on the various fabrics and draw around the outside edge with the pencil. This pencil line is the sewing line. Cut out the fabric pieces, adding a 6 mm/¼ in seam allowance all around each piece.

Piecing

1 Centre a cardboard template on the wrong side of a fabric piece. Turn the seam allowance over on to the cardboard, folding in the corners to form a mitre.

2 Thread a sewing needle and knot the end of the thread. Beginning in the centre of one side of the diamond, baste the seam allowance together around the diamond. (Fig. 1)

3 When all the diamonds have been prepared in this way, you are ready to begin joining them together. Place two diamonds together with right sides facing and the edges even. Diamonds are joined by overcasting across the two adjoining edges of both diamonds. Always choose a sewing thread that matches the darker of the two fabrics you are working with.

Beginning 6 mm/$\frac{1}{4}$ in from the left-hand end of the side you want to sew, work to that end, then down the whole side to the other end, then work backwards for 6 mm/$\frac{1}{4}$ in. (Fig. 2). This method ensures a very secure join which will not come undone. Cut off the thread, leaving a short tail. Take care not to stitch through the cardboard. Piece six matching diamonds together in this way to make the star.

4 Following the block diagram given on page 23, piece all the stars together with the background pieces to form a complete hexagonal unit. Make nine such units. The cardboard should bend quite easily, making your piecing more comfortable to hold as the work grows bigger.

5 Trace and cut the fabric and cardboard, using template C. Baste template C fabric pieces over the cardboard as for the diamonds. Join the template C pieces to each side of the hexagonal unit, using the same method of piecing as for the stars.

6 Following the construction diagram on page 23, lay all the units with the background pieces D, E, F and G on the floor or some other suitable surface. Experiment with the arrangement of the hexagonal units until you are pleased with it, then piece all the elements to form the quilt top.

7 Measure the length of the quilt top through the centre. Cut two 11 cm/4$\frac{1}{2}$ in wide fabric borders to this length plus 12 mm/$\frac{1}{2}$ in for seam allowances. Cut the cardboard to size without seam allowances. If you need to join cardboard to achieve this length do so by butting the edges together – do not overlap them – and secure them with masking tape. Join the side borders in the same way as the stars were pieced. Make the top and bottom borders in the same way.

8 When the quilt top is assembled, remove all the basting and the cardboard. Press well.

9 On the outside edges, redo the basting so that there is a 6 mm/$\frac{1}{4}$ in basted hem all around the quilt top.

Quilting

1 Lay the backing fabric face down on a suitable surface and tape it in place so it does not move. Place the wadding on top and then the completed quilt top on top of that. Note that the backing fabric and the wadding are both bigger than the quilt top – these will be trimmed later. (Fig. 3)

2 Baste from the centre diagonally out to the edges and then in the lines indicated in the diagram. (Fig. 4) Baste around the edges.

3 Quilt the quilt top as you please. Quilting around the stars, hexagonal units and borders is very simple and attractive. Stop the quilting 2.5 cm/1 in from the edges.

4 When the quilting is complete, trim the wadding to the same size as the quilt top.

5 Trim the backing to be 2 cm/$\frac{3}{4}$ in bigger than the quilt top. Fold under this 2 cm/$\frac{3}{4}$ in so that it sits on the front of the wadding between the quilt top and the wadding. Slipstitch the folded edges together.

Don't forget to sign and date your quilt on the back.

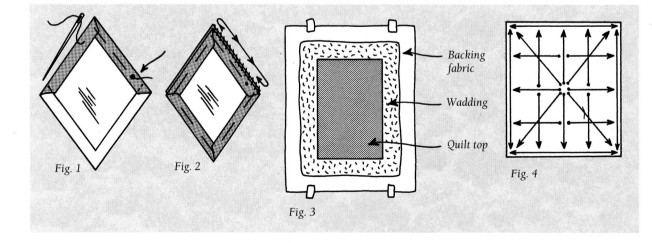

Fig. 1
Fig. 2
Backing fabric
Wadding
Quilt top
Fig. 3
Fig. 4

Block Diagram

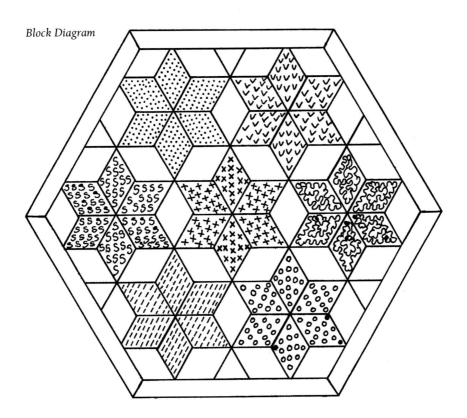

*Construction
Diagram*

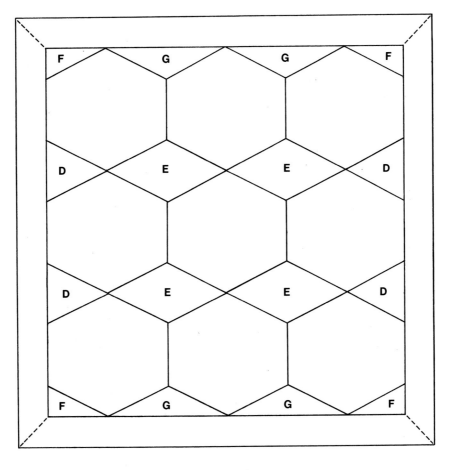

Church Dollies

STITCHED BY HEATHER LAMERTON

In days gone by, mothers, anxious to quieten restless children during the church service, would knot their linen hankerchiefs into a plaything.

Materials

- ♣ two pieces of fine cotton batiste, one 34 cm x 43 cm/13½ in x 17½ in and the other 6 cm x 43 cm/2½ in x 17½ in for the dress and body
- ♣ 10 cm/4 in of fine cotton batiste for the collar and bonnet
- ♣ 1.8 m/2 yd of insertion lace
- ♣ 90 cm/36 in of beading
- ♣ 1.8 m/2 yd of entredeux
- ♣ 70 cm/28 in of edging lace
- ♣ matching sewing thread
- ♣ twin needle
- ♣ pintucking sewing machine foot (optional)
- ♣ water-soluble marker pen
- ♣ 3 mm/⅛ in wide ribbon
- ♣ cotton wool or polyester fibre fill
- ♣ scraps of embroidery yarns for the face and hair

Method

See the Collar Pattern on the Pull Out Pattern Sheet.

1 Press the 6 cm x 43 cm/2½ in x 17½ in piece of batiste in half across the 6 cm/2½ in width. Using the twin needle, make the first pintuck on this fold. Make another pintuck on either side of the first one. Make another three tucks 6mm/¼ in on either side of this first group. Zigzag around the edges of the piece. (Fig. 1)

2 Cut four pieces of insertion, two pieces of beading, and four pieces of entredeux, each 43 cm/17 in long. Cut the batiste from one edge of one length of entredeux and, using a small zigzag stitch, join a piece of insertion to this edge. Next, join a length of beading to the insertion and then join a length of insertion to the beading and finally join on a piece of entredeux trimmed as before. Make two of these panels of joined lace.

3 Trim the batiste from the entredeux on the lace panels. Turn a small hem on the top and bottom of the pintucked piece. Join the trimmed entredeux to the hemmed edges of the batiste with a small zigzag stitch. (Fig. 2)

4 Gather the edging lace by pulling up a thread from the straight edge. Using a small zigzag stitch, attach the gathered edging to one of the lengths of entredeux.

5 On the larger piece zigzag along the 43 cm/17½ in edge, then turn a small hem. Attach this piece to the top edge of the joined piece, using a small zigzag stitch.

6 Round the corners slightly then roll and zigzag all the raw edges, working carefully over the laces.

To form the face

1 With the marker pen, mark the facial features in the centre of the top edge of the fabric, 9 cm/3½ in from the edge. Embroider the face, using appropriately coloured yarns.

2 Fold back approximately 7 cm/3 in at the top so that the face now sits at the top. Make a firm 5 cm/2 in ball of cotton wool or polyester fibre fill and position it behind the face. Secure the fabric around the ball by winding sewing thread around the 'neck'. Make the face and head as smooth as possible.

3 Embroider the hair with loops of embroidery yarn. Tie a knot on each side for the hands.

Collar

Cut two pieces of batiste, using the collar pattern. With right sides together, stitch around the outer edge and along the centre back edges in one continuous 3 mm/⅛ in seam. Turn the collar to the right side. Zigzag the raw edges together. Position the collar on the doll and catch the centre back edges together with a stitch.

Bonnet

1 Cut two pieces of batiste, one 3 cm x 4 cm/1¼ in x 1½ in and the other 2 cm x 12 cm/¾ in x 4¾ in. Roll and zigzag the edges of both pieces.

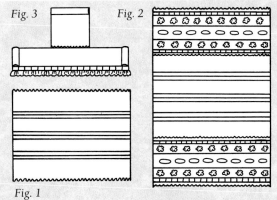

2 On the 3 cm x 4 cm/1¼ in x 1¾ in piece, make a small casing along one 4 cm/1½ in edge. Make two small casings on the 2 cm/¾ in edges of the other piece. Pin the smaller piece to the centre of one of the long sides of the larger piece then zigzag it in place (Fig. 3). Stitch a length of entredeux to the other long side.

3 Gather 24 cm/9½ in of edging lace to fit the length of the entredeux by pulling up a thread in the straight edge. Zigzag the entredeux in place.

4 Thread the silk ribbon through the casings. Pull up the ribbon and tie it in a bow under the 'chin'.

Fig. 3   Fig. 2

Fig. 1

Cabbage Rose Cushion

STITCHED BY GLORIA McKINNON

Lush cabbage roses are romantic and feminine and the perfect decoration for a cushion cover. For a natural look, make the rose from three shades of the one colour, from light to dark.

Materials

- ❧ 75 cm/30 in moire fabric
- ❧ 50 cm/20 in of 2.5 cm/1 in wide double-sided matte ribbon in a dark shade
- ❧ 1 m/40 in of 2.5 cm/1 in wide double-sided matte ribbon in a medium shade
- ❧ 2 m/2 yd of 2.5 cm/1 in wide double-sided matte ribbon in a light shade
- ❧ 50 cm/20 in of 2.5 cm/1 in wide double-sided matte ribbon in green
- ❧ sewing needle, sharp, size 8
- ❧ tapestry needle, size 20
- ❧ embroidery hoop
- ❧ sewing thread in the colour of the cushion
- ❧ green embroidery thread for the stems
- ❧ 30 cm/12 in cushion insert

Method

1 Cut two 28 cm/11¼ in squares for the cushion front and back. Cut three strips for the ruffle, 15 cm x 115 cm/ 6 in x 45 in.

2 Place the cushion cover front in the hoop and pull the fabric taut, then embroider the rose, buds and leaves.

Embroidery

To form the bud

Take a 10 cm/4 in length of ribbon and tie a loose knot in the centre then bring both tails of the knot together underneath the knot. Tease out the loops of the knot a little to adjust the shape of the bud. Cut the tails back to about 1.5 cm/ ¾ in. Stitch the bud to the cushion cover so that the tails lie flat and the bud stands upright.

To form the flower

1 Make a bud in the way described above. Cut four 9 cm/3½ in lengths of the medium shade of ribbon. Fold both ends of each piece down at an angle of 45 degrees. Run a curved line of basting along the lower edge of each length, catching the folded ends in the stitching. Pull up the basting to gather the ribbon, forming petals. Stitch each petal to the base of the bud in a natural-looking arrangement.

2 Make another group of petals in the light-coloured ribbon. You will need six or seven petals in the second row and eight or nine petals in the third row. In the last row, make only four or five petals going only halfway around the rose so that the centre doesn't look like a bullseye.

To form the leaves

Thread the tapestry needle with the green ribbon. Beginning on the wrong side of the cushion cover front, bring the needle up through the fabric close to the base of the rose. Lay the ribbon flat and take a stitch of the desired length (usually about 1 cm/½ in), reinserting the needle through the ribbon itself. This is called 'ribbon stitch' and it is this method which folds the ends of the leaves into a gentle point. When the leaves are in place, stitch lines of stem stitch in green embroidery thread to join the leaves and flowers together.

Assembling

1 Join the short ends of the ruffle strip to form a circle. Fold the strip over double with the wrong sides together. Divide the strip into quarters and mark the quarter points with a pin. Gather the raw edges together. Pin the ruffle around the cushion front, adjusting the gathering and matching the pin marks to the corners. Stitch the ruffle in place.

2 Place the cushion cover front and back together with the right sides facing and the ruffle in between. Stitch in the ruffle stitching line, leaving one side open. Turn the cushion cover to the right side. Place the insert inside the cover and slipstitch the opening closed.

Flower Basket Picture

STITCHED BY BEVERLY SHELDRICK

This charming picture uses the same silk ribbon embroidery techniques as are used on small cushions and the like. The difference is that here they are bold in size, making a terrific impact.

Materials

- ❧ 45 cm/18 in square of linen
- ❧ 30 cm/12 in embroidery hoop
- ❧ an assortment of Piecemaker tapestry needles, sizes 20 to 24
- ❧ silk ribbon in a variety of widths and colours
- ❧ silk embroidery thread in colours to match the ribbon and the basket
- ❧ two gold cherubs
- ❧ sewing thread
- ❧ fine water-soluble marker pen
- ❧ craft glue

Method

See the Basket and Handle Patterns on the Pull Out Pattern Sheet.

Preparation

Using the marker pen, lightly draw in the basket and handle shape on the linen or baste them in with sewing thread. Note that the base of the basket is 7.5 cm/3 in wide and the basket is 5 cm/2 in high. The handle is 16 cm/6½ in high and approximately 11 cm/4½ in wide at its widest point.

Embroidery

For the basket

1 Stitch the basketweave, using 4 mm/^{3}/16 in wide silk ribbon, held in place with tiny French knots in matching silk thread at the intersections of the weaving. The base of the basket is couched over the weaving with a contrasting 7 mm/^{5}/16 in wide silk ribbon.

2 The handle is worked in straight stitches of 7 mm/^{5}/16 in wide silk ribbon in the same colour as the basket, couched over with the same ribbon as the basket base.

For the flowers

Embroider the flowers in a variety of stitches and colours to please yourself, using the stitches described on pages 4 to 6. Use the picture as a guide, if you wish to have something similar, or be daring and design your own.

To finish off

1 Tie a bow in a 130 cm/52 in length of 7 mm/^{3}/16 in wide silk ribbon. Attach the bow and tails over the handle of the basket, using tiny French knots in matching silk embroidery thread to keep the graceful shape of the bow and the bow tails.

2 Glue on the two cherubs, entwining their arms in the ribbon tails.

Découpage Box

MADE BY NERIDA SINGLETON

This box is a beautiful example of découpage – the creative composition of paper cutouts on a surface which is then covered by numerous applications of clear varnish, allowing the image to glow through.

When découpaging a box, always keep the focus of the design on the top and front of the box with less emphasis on the bottom and sides. The background can be painted, covered with wrapping paper or constructed from pictures.

Materials

- ❧ box (with the fittings removed)
- ❧ curved cuticle or surgical scissors, finely pointed
- ❧ 10 cm/4 in rubber roller
- ❧ 2.5 cm/1 in imitation sable brush for varnish
- ❧ Liquitex Gloss Medium and Varnish OR Atelier OR Matisse MM7 OR Jo Sonja Gloss Medium Varnish for Découpage for sealing
- ❧ Clag School Paste and PVA adhesive
- ❧ Goddard's Cabinet Makers Polish
- ❧ Wattyl Danish Wax (optional)
- ❧ sponge applicator or cheap brush for sealer and gesso
- ❧ gesso
- ❧ glass paper
- ❧ wet and dry sandpapers, 280, 600, 1200 and 2000 aluminium oxide
- ❧ clear varnish (various brands of varnish and polyurethanes will do)
- ❧ tack cloth
- ❧ steel wool, 0000
- ❧ Blu-Tack or Faber Castell's Tackit
- ❧ oil-based colouring pencils: sepia, black
- ❧ sponge and towel
- ❧ protective mask and goggles
- ❧ mineral turpentine and brush cleaner
- ❧ beeswax stick or wood putty
- ❧ Scotchbrite scourer
- ❧ brass fittings
- ❧ sheets of no. 10 white cardboard
- ❧ 3M microfine or micromesh finishing kits
- ❧ artists acrylic paints (if you are painting a background), and sea sponge
- ❧ black fineline permanent marker pen OR gold fineline permanent marker pen
- ❧ workable fixative (optional)
- ❧ waxed paper
- ❧ plastic zip folders
- ❧ rubber or cork block
- ❧ scalpel or paring knife
- ❧ muslin cloth
- ❧ craft glue
- ❧ spray adhesive
- ❧ spatula
- ❧ wadding
- ❧ fabric for the lining
- ❧ cutting compound
- ❧ electric drill and 2 mm/ $1/16$ in drill bit
- ❧ ribbon

Method

Preparation

1 Mark the top and bottom of the inside of one side of the box so that it will fit flush when hinged. Check for crevices which may need to be filled with the beeswax stick or wood putty. Apply the filler with the spatula. If you are using putty, be generous with it because it will shrink as it dries. Beeswax is preferable for filling as it does not shrink.

2 Sand the box well with glass paper, then sand it lightly with no. 280 wet and dry sandpaper and wipe it clean.

3 If you wish, you can apply the gesso before lightly sealing the box or you can paint the background with at least two coats of artists acrylic paints, applying each coat in a different direction. If you are not applying gesso or painting the background, eliminate step 3.

4 Seal the box with your choice of sealer, drawing the sealer out well so that no bumps and lumps are evident. Seal the inside and rims of the box as well.

5 Seal the images sparingly on both sides of the paper before cutting them out. Seal the back of the picture first. Allow it to dry for ten to fifteen minutes, then sparingly seal the front of the picture.

6 Cut out each picture precisely, eliminating the inside areas you don't need before cutting the outline. Cut with the curve of the scissors pointing away from the picture. Remove all the white background at the edges of the image.

7 Make a cardboard template for each surface of the box. Using the Blu-Tack, experiment with the design, beginning with the focal picture and building up the complementary images until you are satisfied with the effect.

Note: Pictures which cover a corner and travel down the sides will have to be mitred at the corners. Make sure you have enough pictures before you begin gluing.

Gluing

1 Using a 3:1 mixture of Clag paste and PVA apply a generous amount to the box surface and smear it with your fingertips until it is silky. Before placing the pictures down, make sure that you have not missed any areas and that there are no hard lumps of glue. Place the first picture, then massage with a little extra glue on top of the picture until the glue becomes tacky and the bonding between the picture and surface takes place. Distribute the glue evenly behind each picture.

2 Add a little more glue, then using the rubber roller, roll with very gentle pressure from the centre of the picture out to the edges. Don't use too much pressure when you are rolling as this will eliminate all the glue and you will have no adhesion. Hold the surface up to the light to check if there is any accumulated glue or air behind the picture. Keep the roller clean by wiping off built-up glue.

3 Using a damp sponge, wipe any excess glue from the surface of the picture. The glue will appear dull when held in the light. Do not glue over a wet picture.

4 Repeat steps 1 to 4 until all the pictures have been glued down. Check that there are no dull patches.

5 Allow the box to dry, then check each picture for white edges. Colour any that you find with an appropriately coloured oil-based pencil and smudge the edge if the line is too definite. This will allow all the images to blend together.

6 Sign and date your work with the marker pen. If you are using a gold fineline pen, spray your signature sparingly with workable fixative when the ink is dry, otherwise it will smear under the sealer. Allow the fixative to dry.

7 Seal all the surfaces sparingly. If you are not able to finish gluing and have to leave the project overnight, clear away all the glue, pencil any edges, then seal the object. This will prevent the pictures from losing adhesion, especially at the corners, and also alleviates the possibility of damage. (Vermin are instantly attracted to the excess glue on the pictures.)

8 If you do not use all the sealed pictures, place them between sheets of waxed paper and file them into plastic zip folders. The sealer will stick them together if you don't use the waxed papers to separate them.

Varnishing

1 Use the protective mask and have good ventilation in the area in which you are working, when you are varnishing. Using the fine brush, beginning applying the varnish at the top, using light sweeps in one direction. Do not stir the varnish or polyurethane unless so advised in the manufacturer's instructions. Satin, matte and water-based products should be thoroughly stirred to incorporate the sediment. Gloss is a harder and more suitable product.

2 Be sure to brush out any accumulation of varnish where the top and sides of the box join or at the rims. Check for drips. Wipe the excess varnish from the brush on to the side of the varnish tin. Using the tip of the brush, lightly sweep across all the surfaces to remove any air bubbles and excess varnish. Be sure to work in a good light. Support both sections of the box raised on tins to allow the air to circulate around them while they dry.

3 Allow twenty-four hours drying time between each coat of varnish. Before applying the next coat of varnish, wipe the surface dust particles off with the tack cloth. Alternate the direction of each coat of varnish.

4 When you have applied twenty coats, begin sanding with the no. 600 wet and dry sandpaper. Sand lightly in one direction with the wet sandpaper wrapped around a rubber or a cork block. Wipe off the white residue with the damp sponge then allow the box to dry. Colour any white edges, then seal the surfaces and begin varnishing again.

5 Repeat the process of sanding with the no. 600 wet and dry sandpaper and varnishing until the surface is quite flat. This may take somewhere between thirty and fifty coats of varnish.

6 Change to no. 1200 sandpaper for the final polishing after the last three coats of varnish have been applied. Remove the excess build-up of varnish at the rims of the box using a scalpel or paring knife. Be sure the surface is uniformly dull – that there are no crevices between superimposed pictures which show tendrils of gloss. If there is still gloss evident, rub with a dry Scotchbrite, then with the steel wool. A cutting compound is also helpful at this stage.

7 For a gloss finish, apply a light coat of varnish, using seven parts varnish to three parts mineral turpentine. Be sure there are no air bubbles in the surface and place the object in a dust-free environment to dry. Repeat this process until the surface is perfectly smooth.

8 For a waxed finish, put a teaspoon each of clear beeswax and the Goddard's polish in an oven to warm them, or in a microwave oven for about twenty seconds on HIGH. Apply the polish sparingly with the dampened muslin cloth and work on only small sections at a time. Dip the cloth in boiling water and buff each section before you move on to the next one. Repeat if necessary. Apply a final light coat of the polish over the entire surface and repeat this often during the curing time to enhance the finish even further. It can take from six to twelve months for an object to harden completely.

Finishing

1 Using the electric drill and 2 mm/ ^{1}/16 in bit, secure the brass corners. Avoid fittings which are secured with nails – those with screws are the most suitable. Use the drill bit for all the fittings, starting with the corners. Work on the handle and then the top. You will find it easier to manipulate the fittings before the hinges are attached.

To attach the hinges, measure an equal distance from the ends and drill the opposite sides in sequence. Add the clasp – choose one that has a padlock. It is best to secure the top of the clasp and then line up the underneath section to ensure it is not too loose. An antique padlock and handles can add a great deal of style to a box.

2 If you have not taken the pictures over the rim, paint the inside of the box rims with artists acrylic paints. Leave to dry, then apply two coats of sealer, allowing time for the paint to dry between each coat.

Lining

1 Cut ten cardboard shapes for templates, remembering to allow for the thickness of the fabric at each side. Cut 6 mm/ ^{1}/4 in of wadding the same size as the top and bottom templates. Lightly spray the cardboard with the spray adhesive and stick the wadding to the cardboard.

2 Cut the fabric 1.5 cm/ ^{3}/4 in wider than the template all around. Mitre the corners by cutting a triangle from each corner of the fabric to allow it to fit flush at the corners when glued. Glue the edges of the fabric to the back of the cardboard with craft glue. Apply the craft glue to the bottom of the box, spreading it evenly with a spatula. Place the fabric-covered template on to the glue and weight it down to ensure adhesion.

3 Now that the thickness of the cardboard, wadding and fabric is determined in the top and bottom of the box, reduce the width of the cardboard templates accordingly for all the sides. The length of the sides will also need to accommodate two thicknesses of extra fabric so keep readjusting them. Do not pad the sides as this will reduce the interior space of the box. Attach the fabric-covered side pieces in the same way as for the top and bottom, but omitting the wadding. Work on each side separately. Secure the sides with craft glue keeping pressure on them until they are firmly stuck. Glue a length of ribbon behind the covered cardboard on one end to hold the box lid open. It is a good idea to do these two ends last.

4 If your box is round or oval with the lip of the lid fitting over the base, make a pencil line around the base of the lip on to the bottom and only paste the pictures to this line. Successive coats of varnish will build up and prevent the lid from fitting properly. The bare areas can be painted in a colour to match the background colour of the pictures or in a colour which coordinates with the lining.

Nerida Singleton has written three découpage books:

♣ *Découpage,* Boolarong Publications, Brisbane 1990
♣ *Découpage, An Illustrated Guide,* Sally Milner Publishing, 1991
♣ *Découpage Designs,* Sally Milner Publishing, 1992, and a calendar
♣ *Découpage Calendar,* Five Mile Press & Sally Milner Publishing, 1993

Cream-on-Cream Blanket

STITCHED BY MARG MANNING

What an exquisite piece this is. Rather than the embroidery contrasting with the wool fabric, this blanket features the delicate effect of cream on cream, accentuated by cream lace and ribbons. You might like to experiment with monochromatic schemes of your own.

Materials

- ✿ 80 cm x 115 cm/32 in x 45 in cream blanket wool
- ✿ 8 m/9 yd of 8 cm/3¼ in wide cream edging lace
- ✿ 4 m/4½ yd of beading
- ✿ 6 m/6⅔ yd of 7 mm/⁵⁄₁₆ in wide cream silk ribbon
- ✿ 80 cm/32 in of Vyella for the backing
- ✿ a variety of wools and threads for the embroidery
- ✿ matching sewing thread
- ✿ suitable embroidery and sewing needles
- ✿ tracing paper and pencil (optional)
- ✿ bodkin

Method

See the Embroidery Design on the Pull Out Pattern Sheet.

1 Fold the blanket in half lengthwise and widthwise to find the centre. Mark this point.

2 Baste the outline of the heart on to the blanket, centring it over the middle point. You may wish to trace the outline before you baste it to ensure the heart has a good shape.

3 Embroider the flowers around the heart, using the stitches indicated on the embroidery guide. However, don't feel bound by these stitches – use them as a guide only. You may like to experiment with the different threads and wools to decide which one best suits which flower.

4 Join the ends of the edging lace to form a circle. Gather up the straight edge of the lace to fit around the embroidered wool fabric. Pin the lace around the embroidered wool fabric with the straight edge of the lace along the edge of the wool. Adjust the gathers and stitch the lace into place, either by hand or by machine.

5 Place the embroidered wool fabric and the Vyella together with the right sides facing, the raw edges even and the lace sandwiched in between. Stitch around the outside edge with a 1 cm/½ in seam allowance, leaving a 15 cm/6 in opening in one side. Take care not to catch the lace in the stitching. Turn the blanket through to the right side. Slipstitch the opening closed.

6 Handsew the beading around the edge of the front of the blanket. Cut the silk ribbon into four lengths, two 1.75 m/2 yd long and two 1.25 m/ 50 in long. Thread the ribbon through the beading from corner to corner, using the bodkin. Tie the ribbon into a bow at each corner. You can work a French knot on the knot of the bow to keep it flat and in place.

Paper Tole Picture

MADE BY GLORIA MCKINNON

Paper tole is a traditional craft which is currently enjoying a great revival. Different elements are cut out of identical pictures and are then layered to give a realistic three-dimensional effect.

This really is a project anyone can do and the results will be enjoyed for years to come.

It is a good idea to have your picture professionally framed to give it a perfect finishing touch.

Materials

- ❧ six Mollie Brett Nursery Rhyme Prints
- ❧ craft knife or scalpel
- ❧ self-healing cutting mat
- ❧ 20 cm x 24 cm/8 in x 9½ in backing board
- ❧ tube of silicone
- ❧ pencil
- ❧ tweezers
- ❧ toothpicks
- ❧ spray adhesive
- ❧ hi-gloss varnish and thinner
- ❧ small brush
- ❧ Faber Castell Studio Marker, grey

Method

Note: Pieces are shaped before being attached, to give them a more realistic look. To shape, place the cut-out piece in your cupped hand and roll the scalpel handle or another cylindrical object across it.

On the backing board, draw a circle the same size as the picture, leaving a 4.5 cm/1¾ in space at the top.

Sheet 1

1 Using the craft knife or scalpel and the cutting mat, cut out the upper oven, including the rabbit's head; the lower oven, including the dough; and the doorway. Place the remainder of the picture on the circle on the backing board and lightly mark the positions of the cut-out pieces with the pencil. Set this part of the picture aside – it could be useful later if you make a mistake with another part.

2 Glue the cut-out pieces accurately into position using the spray adhesive. Use the tweezers and the toothpicks to help you position the pieces.

Sheet 2

1 Cut out the upper oven again, but this time do not include the rabbit's head; cut out the lower oven again, excluding the dough; and cut out the doorway again.

2 On the part of the picture that remains, shape the door frame and the oven opening slightly inwards to give added dimension to the oven and door. Glue it in place over the stuck-down pieces on the backing, using the spray adhesive. Take care not to flatten the shaping.

Sheet 3

1 Cut around the baker's shovel, the table legs, the bread and tray and all four rabbits in one piece. Colour all the cut edges with the marker pen.

2 Attach the baker's shovel to the backing picture with a blob of silicone at the top and at the bottom.

3 Attach the rabbits, using blobs of silicone on the end of a toothpick at 1 cm/½ in intervals as the piece is quite long. Attach the bread and tray.

4 Fold the front table leg lengthwise to shape it, then attach it with silicone. Attach the other table leg.

Sheet 4

1 Cut out the four rabbits in one piece, leaving off the legs of the bench, the feet and the right arm of the mother rabbit and the feet of the baker bunny. Cut out the bread without the tray. Colour the cut edges as before.

2 Shape the bread so it sits slightly forward, then attach it with silicone.

3 Attach the rabbits with blobs of silicone placed at 1 cm/½ in intervals across the piece.

Sheet 5

1 Cut out the baker's hat and the rabbit's ear. Cut out and colour the edges of the cuffs of the baker's pants. Cut out the tin on the left, the bread dough, the head, ribbon, cape and arm of the mother rabbit, the small rabbit in the red beret without the feet and tail, the cooked bread, the assistant baker without the tail and the arm holding the tray, the baker's sleeve, the baker's shirt, the baker's pants. Colour all the edges and shape.

2 Attach all the pieces with appropriate numbers of silicone blobs.

Sheet 6

1 Cut out the baker's head, the small rabbit's head and arm and left front of pants, the assistant's yellow cuff, the green bow tie and the arm and sleeve holding the cake tray, the two rows of cakes on the tray, the baker's apron and ties, the baker's tail. Colour all the edges and shape.

2 Attach all the pieces with appropriate numbers of silicone blobs.

Finishing

Coating the assembled picture with a gloss is optional, but as the aim is to make the finished paper look like tin, I always add varnish.

1 Load the brush with a small amount of the hi-gloss thinner, then load the brush with the varnish. The thinner allows the varnish to go on more evenly. Apply two coats, allowing the varnish to dry between coats.

2 Have your picture framed professionally with a suitably coloured mat and the little verse underneath.

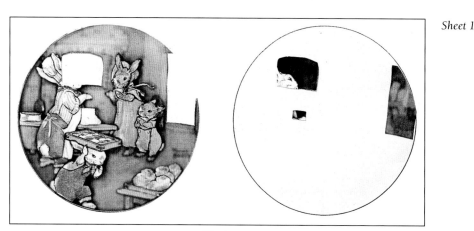

Sheet 1

Sheet 2

Sheet 3

Sheet 4

Sheet 5

Sheet 6

Twilight Garden Quilt

STITCHED BY YAN PRING WITH THANKS TO MARY ELLEN HOPKINS

This is a quick little quilt to make. Machine-pieced and machine-quilted, it simply uses star blocks set on the diagonal, with floating triangles to complete the edges.

You can piece the star blocks with different fabrics for the star points or use the same fabric. The instructions given here are for using the same fabric, but do not be afraid to experiment to achieve a special effect or to include a favourite scrap. It is best to choose the fabrics for the borders after you have pieced the stars in order to determine what colour will work best with the overall scheme.

Finished size: 104 cm x 125 cm/41 in x 49 in

Materials

- ❧ 1.2 m/1⅓ yd of background fabric
- ❧ 40 cm/½ yd of fabric for the star points
- ❧ 20 cm/¼ yd of fabric for the star centres
- ❧ 20 cm/¼ yd of striped fabric for the inner border
- ❧ 10 cm/4 in of fabric for the middle border
- ❧ 60 cm/¾ yd of floral fabric for the outer border
- ❧ 45 cm/18 in of fabric for the binding
- ❧ 1.3 m/52 in of fabric for the quilt backing
- ❧ 110 cm x 130 cm/44 in x 52 in of wadding
- ❧ transparent ruler
- ❧ sharp pencil
- ❧ scissors, or Olfa cutter and self-healing mat
- ❧ pins
- ❧ matching sewing threads
- ❧ masking tape

Method

See the Construction Diagram on the Pull Out Pattern Sheet.

Cutting

Note: 6 mm/¼ in seam allowances are included in all the measurements. Be exact with your seam allowances, otherwise the quilt will not come together well. It is a good idea to place all the pieces into piles marked A, B, C, D, E.

Cut out the following pieces:

From the background fabric: Seventeen squares (A), 11 cm x 11 cm/4¼ in x 4¼ in; forty-eight rectangles (B), 7.5 cm x 11 cm/3 in x 4¼ in; four squares (C), 23 cm x 23 cm/9 in x 9 in, cut into quarters diagonally; two squares (D), 18 cm x 18 cm/7 in x 7 in, cut in half diagonally; three squares (E), 11 cm x 11 cm/4¼ in x 4¼ in, cut into quarters diagonally.

From the star point fabric: one hundred and forty-four squares 4.5 cm x 4.5 cm/1¾ in x 1¾ in.

From the star centre fabric: eighteen squares 7.5 cm x 7.5 cm/3 in x 3 in.

From the striped border fabric: four 4.5 cm/1¾ in wide strips across the full width of the fabric.

From the middle border fabric: four 2.5 cm/1 in wide strips across the full width of the fabric.

From the floral border fabric: four 14.5 cm/5¾ in wide strips across the full width of the fabric.

Piecing

1 Lay one of the star point squares in the upper left-hand corner of one of the background rectangles B with the right sides together and the raw edges even. Stitch across the diagonal. (Fig. 1) Trim off the upper triangle of the star point square and press the remaining triangle over to the right side. (Fig. 2)

2 Make twenty-four such rectangles with a triangle in two corners (Fig. 3) and twenty-four with four triangles. (Fig. 4)

3 Assemble the quilt, following the construction diagram. First assemble diagonal strips (including the triangles at the ends) until you have all thirteen strips as numbered on the diagram and press. Next, join the strips together horizontally and press. Press the quilt top well.

For the borders

1 For the striped inner border, join the two side borders first, then trim them to fit the edges of the quilt top. Attach the top and bottom borders in the same way. Press.

GARDENING TOOLS FROM MORRIS HOME AND GARDEN WARES, CHATSWOOD, NSW

2 Attach the middle border and then the outer border in the same way. Press. (Fig. 5)

Quilting

1 Lay the backing fabric face down on a suitable surface and tape it in place so it does not move. Place the wadding on top and then the completed quilt top on top of that. Note that the backing and the wadding are both bigger than the quilt top – these will be trimmed later.

2 Baste from the centre out to the edges and then in the lines indicated in the diagram. (Fig. 6) Baste around the edges.

3 Machine-quilt following the diagonal lines of the piecing. The two narrow borders are quilted in the ditch, following the seams.

4 Handquilt the floral border in a random pattern, outlining the flowers in the print.

5 When the quilting is completed, trim the backing and the wadding to the same size as the quilt top.

Binding

1 Cut six 7 cm/3 in wide strips of the binding fabric. Join the six strips to achieve the required length.

2 Fold the strip over double with wrong sides together and raw edges even. Press.

3 Pin the binding around the right side of the quilt with the raw edge of the binding 6 mm/¼ in from the quilt edge. Stitch in a 6 mm/¼ in seam.

4 Press the binding over to the back of the quilt and either machine-sew or handsew the binding in place.

Don't forget to sign and date your quilt on the back.

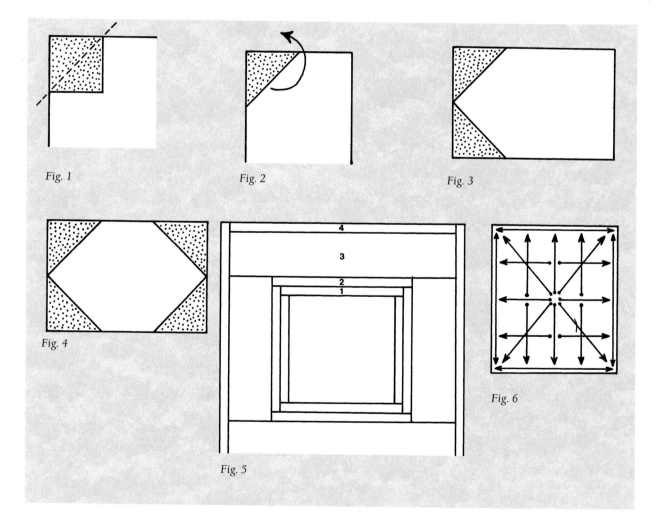

Fig. 1

Fig. 2

Fig. 3

Fig. 4

Fig. 5

Fig. 6

Lisel Heeps who made this charming topiary picture was first introduced to this technique by Kathleen Mathews, a dried flower artist. It is made in a very similar way to the one on page 46, except that you will need to create a base for the flower ball from twigs. When you have attached the half pot and trunk, glue four 7 cm/3 in twigs into an open square at the top of the trunk. Glue the dried flowers over this frame until you have a nice round shape.

Embroidered Cushions

MADE BY GLORIA McKINNON

A heart-shaped garland of silk ribbon flowers is the perfect foil for a ruffled cushion. For a dramatic effect, embroider it on a black linen cushion and embellish it with a cherub. The same embroidery creates a totally different effect on a rich gold brocade cushion or framed as a picture.

Materials

For each cushion:
- ♣ 60 cm/24 in of 150 cm/60 in wide fabric
- ♣ silk ribbon in various colours and widths
- ♣ matching sewing thread
- ♣ an assortment of Piecemaker tapestry needles, sizes 20 and 22, and crewel needles, size 8
- ♣ tailors chalk
- ♣ tracing paper and pencil
- ♣ 24 cm/9 ½ in cushion insert or polyester fibre fill
- ♣ bread dough or sculptured cherub

Method

See the Embroidery Guide and the Heart Pattern on the Pull Out Pattern Sheet.

Embroidery

1 Cut two 20 cm/8 in squares from the fabric for the cushion front and back.

2 Fold one square of linen into quarters and mark the centre. Trace the heart pattern, cut it out and draw the outline centred over the middle point. Baste around the shape of the heart.

3 Embroider the flowers around the heart, using the stitches and ribbon indicated in the embroidery guide and on pages 4 to 7. When the embroidery is complete, glue on the cherub.

Assembling

1 Cut two strips 20 cm x 150 cm/8 in x 60 in for the ruffle. Sew the ends together to form a circle. Fold the ruffle strip over double with wrong sides together and raw edges even. Divide the length of the ruffle into quarters and mark them with pins.

2 Gather up the ruffle and pin it to the right side of the embroidered linen with raw edges even and the pins placed at the corners. Adjust the gathering. Baste then stitch the ruffle into place.

3 Fold the ruffle over on to the embroidered fabric. Place the cushion front and back pieces together with right sides facing. Stitch around the outside edge in the stitching line of the ruffle, leaving an opening on one side for turning. Turn the cushion through to the right side.

4 Place the insert inside the cover or stuff the cover quite firmly with the fibre fill, then slipstitch the opening closed.

If you are making the embroidered picture, embroider a square of fabric in the same way as for the cushion. Press around the embroidery so as not to flatten it, before framing it yourself or having it framed professionally.

Floral Foursome

MADE BY GLORIA McKINNON

Terracotta and pine give a warm 'country' feel to this dried flower wall picture which would look great in a sunny kitchen or family room.

Materials

- ❧ 40 cm x 70 cm/16 in x 28 in pine backboard or ten 7 cm wide x 40 cm long /3 in wide x 16 in long tongue and groove boards to make your own backboard
- ❧ four lengths of mitred pine, two pieces 7 cm x 40 cm/3 in x 16 in and two pieces 7 cm x 70 cm/3 in x 28 in, for the frame
- ❧ two 10 cm/4 in terracotta pots or four half terracotta pots
- ❧ small block of oasis
- ❧ dried flowers, such as lavender, roses, daisies, larkspur
- ❧ 75 cm/30 in wired ribbon
- ❧ 3 m/3¼ yd raffia
- ❧ small amount of moss
- ❧ wood glue or hammer and nails
- ❧ wire and ring hooks for hanging
- ❧ hot melt glue gun

Method

1 If you are making your own backboard, glue or nail the tongue and groove boards together.

2 Nail or glue the lengths of mitred pine together to form a frame. Nail or glue the frame to the backboard.

3 If you are using the 10 cm/4 in terracotta pots, cut them in half. Using the glue gun, glue the half pots in a straight line across the backboard at the marked points. Place the pots so that they appear to be resting on the top edge of the bottom of the frame. Glue a small piece of oasis into each of the pots.

4 Push the flower stems into the oasis, taking care to keep them straight. When all the flowers are in place, glue a little moss around the base of the flowers, covering the oasis.

5 Tie bows from the ribbon and from the raffia and glue them to the front of the pots.

Acknowledgments

I would like to begin by apologising to every needlecraft author. I always wondered why they had to thank EVERYONE. I now know why: you need to and, what's more, you really want to.

My very special thanks go to:

Anne O'Brien, whose idea it was to open the store in the first place; our 'friends of the store' – customers, students and teachers; my store manager, Fay King, and staff past and present; my family for their support; for their special help with the projects in this book, teachers Wendy Lee Ragan, Merope Mills and Nerida Singleton; all the visiting teachers from the United States, England, New Zealand and Australia, for their wonderful enthusiasm and input; Martha Pullen for a long and happy relationship; Judith Montano, because her book *The Art of Silk Embroidery* was our 'coming out', and Rob James and Judy Poulos of J.B. Fairfax Press for their support of this book.

All the products shown in this book are available from
Anne's Glory Box
60-62 Beaumont Street,
Hamilton, Newcastle, NSW 2303
Phone: (049) 61 6016 or Fax: (049) 61 6587

Editorial
Managing Editor: Judy Poulos
Editorial Assistant: Ella Martin
Editorial Coordinator: Margaret Kelly

Photography
Andrew Payne

Styling
Louise Owens, Anne-Maree Unwin

Illustrations
Lesley Griffith

Design and Production
Managers: Sheridan Carter, Anna Maguire
Design and Layout: Jenny Pace

Published by J.B. Fairfax Press Pty Limited
80-82 McLachlan Ave
Rushcutters Bay, NSW 2011
Australia
A.C.N. 003 738 430
Formatted by J.B. Fairfax Press Pty Limited
Printed by Toppan Printing Co, Singapore

JBFP 333

ANNE'S GLORY BOX
Series ISBN 1 86343 166 7
Book 1 ISBN 1 86343 168 3